Giving from their Love Language

The Secrets to Gifts They Love

Linda Johnson

ANGELICO BOOKS

Other books by Linda Johnson

Intuition: Your Most Powerful Tool

Develop your intuition and notice how quickly you become more happy, healthy and wealthy. This simple program helps you understand the source of your intuition and strengthen this critical skill to be more successful at work, in relationships and at home.

http://amzn.to/2eiZlpV

How to Talk to Your Kids and Grandkids: 10 Secrets to being the Grandmothr Everyone Adores

This guide explores the 10 ways to talk to your kids, as well as fun tips for opening up conversations with your grandkids.

http://amzn.to/2ejBNFR

Deborah Williams and Linda A. Johnson

How to Talk to your Kids and Grandkids

10 Secrets to Being the Grandmother Everyone Adores

Beginning Meditation for Busy People: How to Get More Done, Feel Less Stressed and Be Happier

Stress has become a large part of our every day life, making us anxious, exhausted and sometimes even affecting our health. This simple meditation book takes you step-by-step through meditation practices that are designed with a busy lifestyle in mind.
http://amzn.to/2do11n7

The 7 Secrets to Happiness: How to Bring Joy into Your Everyday Life

Happiness seems like a universal desire – lots of people are searching for it, and few really find it. The 7 Secrets of Happiness gives you a clear map for the journey. With simple and powerful life strategies you can easily incorporate into your everyday life to feel more fulfilled, less anxious, and happier!
http://amzn.to/2cPnBBc

TABLE OF CONTENTS

CHAPTER 1

How do you find the perfect gift for your loved ones?

Do you want to give your partner, parents, kids and other loved ones the perfect gifts? The gifts that bring a big grin to their faces and show them how much you really care?

Would you like to be able to express love to the people you care about so that they really, totally *get* how much you care?

Do you want to feel loved and cherished in return?

Do you want to have relationships filled with love that last and last? Do you want to amaze your loved ones with expressions of love they will treasure for a lifetime?

Sounds like a lot? Surprisingly, it's actually quite easy when you give gifts based on love styles.

In this book we're going to talk a bit about love styles and how you determine your partners love style, then give you 57 very concrete types of gifts you can give your loved ones based on love styles. If you are one of those people who want to just jump to the list, click here. But to get the most out of this book, read through the whole thing. It's quite short and to the point!

Ever tried to express your love... and it didn't work?

Since you're reading this book, I know you really want your loved ones to light up when you give to them. Yet you may have had some negative experiences – putting a lot of effort into doing something special for a loved one, only for it to be unappreciated, or even worse, for them to burst into tears.

I know. I've had it happen to me, and my clients have told me stories like this over and over. We put ourselves – time, energy, love – into an expression of love... only to be told that it's not enough. It's sad and frustrating, and ultimately many people just give up.

So, what's going on?

In many instances you and your loved one are using different styles. Love styles, that is.

What is a love style?

Your love style is the primary way that you *express* and *receive* love and affection.

Each of your loved ones *also* has a love style or styles — preferred ways *they* express and receive love.

For each person, their love style is the strongest way that messages of love get through. There are *other* ways that people express love — *ways that would work just fine for someone else* — that *won't* work well for that person. If they were a TV, they'd be tuned to a different channel. Their loved ones are broadcasting love signals, but they're just not receiving.

How can someone not "get it" when you express your love?

Let's start with *your* experience, because it's what you understand from the inside.

No matter how much others *try* to express their love, you will only really "get it" and *feel* it when they use *your* style(s) of loving.

Have you ever wondered how you can be with one or more people you love, and still feel lonely, needy, or unloved? That's how! They may be expressing love as strongly as they know how in *their* styles... but you can only receive love in *your* style. It's like you're starving... and they keep offering you a warm blanket. You need food!

But they *don't* need food. Unlike you, they're comfortably full, but cold. If you try to express love by giving them what would please you – food – it won't work. They'll feel unloved because they really need that warm blanket.

That's how you can express love for all you're worth, yet have a loved one claim they just don't feel loved, wanted, or appreciated. You're saying "I love you" in a language *they don't understand.*

This problem has destroyed millions of relationships. But you're about to take your first step to solving it forever.

You can have relationships like you've dreamed of

Imagine, for a moment, giving your loved one that unconditional love you feel in the exact way they need to feel loved and secure in your relationship.

Imagine now how you would feel if your loved one could do the same – express their unconditional love in a way that you understand and *feel.*

Think of how much richer and loving *all* your relationships could be. Your relationship with your children, your parents, your friends, and especially with your partner.

If you think this is just "pie in the sky" thinking straight from some romance novel, think again. There is absolutely no reason why your relationship — the one you entered with such hope, with such optimism — needs to be damaged or destroyed by a failure to communicate.

In addition, taking this extra effort to understand what makes your partner feel most loved, will provide lasting benefits on the health and longevity of your relationship. It'll probably even improve your sex life (we all know that the brain is our biggest sex organ, and feeling truly loved and understood is a big turn-on).

There's no reason why your love story can't end like it began, like a romance novel. And we all know that every good romance novel ends with a "happily ever after."

From a dying marriage to renewed love

Sound impossible? Trust me, it isn't!

How can I be so sure? Because I turned *my own* relationship around... then helped over 200 couples do the same.

I was on the edge of despair, ready to give up on the love of my life, simply because we had different love styles — and didn't know it. Both my husband and I were *trying* to express love in the strongest ways we knew. But because our love styles differed, both of us ended up feeling frustrated and *unloved*.

We were close to divorcing when someone told me about a book called *The 5 Love Languages*, written by Dr. Gary Chapman. Chapman's theory is that we all have different ways of expressing and receiving love, which he calls *love languages*. One person might feel really loved when they get a physical gift, whereas someone else might see that as a mere token and only really feel loved when they are told "I love you" or given a great hug.

With this information I finally broke through the love barrier and was able to translate what my husband was trying to express when he spoke certain words or gave me gifts or tried to help me in various ways. I was also able to greatly improve my relationships with my children, grandchildren, and friends. I learned that my love style is Practical Assistance. My husband needs *words* of love, and our daughter needs loving touch.

Soon I started working with my clients using Chapman's theory. While I was able to help most of the couples I worked with, it wasn't until I updated and expanded Chapman's ideas that I became able to help virtually *every* couple with their love relationship. The key turned out to be *practical* ideas for expressing love that people could use — like recipes in a cookbook for love! This is the book you're reading now.

I have had tremendous success in assisting people by helping them understand how to give and receive love – to their partners, children, parents, friends, and other loved ones.

What can you achieve using the love styles?

Countless couples have had the spark in their relationships re-lit with this new understanding.

- One couple who had been married for 30 years and were considering divorce are now loving each other like star-struck teenagers because they understand how to give and receive love.

- A couple who had been together less than a year were having regular battles. While they desperately wanted to stay together, both felt fundamentally unloved. Understanding the love styles turned their relationship around.

- One woman who regularly felt sad, unloved, and completely unsupported in her relationship used these techniques to communicate with her husband about what she needed, and finally got the love and support that she desired.

These are just some of the success stories that come with understanding love styles and using them in your relationship.

It doesn't matter what stage your relationship is in. Couples who have experienced 20 years or more of a stale union have taken this incredible, eye-opening system and revitalized their lives. They discovered a new sense of love, a stronger connection, and they experienced the fun and delight that brought them together originally.

Parents who were at their wits' end dealing with difficult children have used the love styles to turn their relationships with their kids around. Other people have created astonishing closeness with friends, estranged relatives, and their parents.

When you discover the secrets to giving each of your loved ones exactly what they want to receive, you'll be delighted to learn that even a little effort on your part produces amazing results towards building that ultimate loving bond.

I guarantee that when you figure out how to show them you love them, your new way of giving will leave lasting loving memories and create a love story that will be told time and time again.

Discover the best-kept secrets of loving couples

Are you ready to turn your love life around? Are you ready to experience the love you once felt for that special person? Heal your relationship with your child? Become closer to your friends?

Right about now you probably have many questions about this process. "Where can I go to learn these love styles? Are they difficult to use? How do we, as a couple, use them to maximize our love?"

That's exactly why I wrote this book. In these pages, you'll discover the answers to the most fundamental questions and concerns many couples including you and your loved one face every single day. I'll reveal the best-kept secrets that the happiest and most loving couples, families, and friends already know.

- Learn what the six love styles are.

- Discover which style you use most often.

- Discover the style each of your loved ones uses. The one you need to learn to create that loving, unshakable bond.

- Learn how to translate your actions and words into the style your loved ones can best understand.

- Get practical ideas on how to give to others in their love style.

Once you learn a new style of expressing love, you become good at it by using it. That's why most of this book is dedicated to increasing your fluency and skill in expressing love in whatever styles each of your loved ones uses. I want nothing more than for you to be successful — wildly successful — in filling your life with love.

Common myths about loving

Before we dive into the love styles, I want to take a moment to dispel some common myths about giving and receiving love that can really hurt your relationships.

If you love someone, you'll "just know" how to express love in the right ways. Wrong! That myth has killed countless marriages and relationships.

The truth is that *none* of us are mind-readers. When we are in rapport with someone, we can *feel* we are reading their mind or they are reading ours. However, research has shown this isn't actually true. We may think and feel *approximately* what our loved one does, but it's not *exactly* the same. Those things we *don't* get right are exactly the things that can cause troubles in our relationships!

This means that your best course of action is to (a) *ask* your loved ones how they like to receive love, (b) *observe* how they respond to love delivered in various love styles, and (c) *express* love to them in the ways that mean the most *to them.*

Your loved ones should know how to love you. Nope. Your loved ones aren't mind readers. That means you need to *clearly* communicate what you want so they can love you the way you want to be loved.

Expressions of love you ask for "don't count." A lot of women especially fall into the trap of wanting their loved ones to *spontaneously* do the things they want, without having to ask. That might be reasonable *after* the giver knows what to deliver, and the receiver has coached the giver long enough that the giver consistently gets things right. It's certainly not realistic to expect it right away.

Expecting your loved ones to read your mind — or worse, getting angry at them for making you ask for what you want — is a sure road to relationship problems.

Frankly, if you want love expressed to you in a particular way, the best way to get it is to ask! Of course you'll get much better results if you make sure your loved ones are getting love in the ways they prefer. You see, when people feel loved, they naturally become more loving.

If you're not getting what you want, make things unpleasant. You're miserable, so you might as well make *them* miserable and motivate them to give you what you want, right? Wrong! Making others feel bad destroys trust and builds resentment and hostility.

According to a lot of research, my personal experience, and the experience of hundreds of my clients, you get *much* better results by *rewarding* people and giving *positive* feedback.

If they're only giving you 1% of what you want, express your delight and appreciation for that 1%, and ignore the 99% as best you can. The more attention and appreciation you give to the behaviors you *do* want, the more likely people are to *want* to do them. Pretty soon that 1% becomes 2%, then 5%, then 20%... It always amazes me how well and how fast rewards can turn a relationship around. Just make sure your positive feedback is in a form that *they* find rewarding. Someone who blossoms if touched may not respond to verbal praise, and vice versa.

The myths above have wrecked countless relationships. This book is all about a better alternative — a way of loving that has saved thousands of marriages and made millions of people happier than they ever dreamed possible.

CHAPTER 2

What are love styles?

You're about to learn the six very different ways individuals *express love* and *receive love.*

It's important to realize that none of these styles is "right" or "wrong," and none is "better" than another.

What *can* cause problems, though, is if people's ways of expressing and receiving love mismatch – and they don't know it. Both people can end up feeling frustrated, unappreciated, and unloved.

Love styles are subtle. When you speak English and someone else speaks Italian, you both *know* you don't speak the same language. Together you make adjustments, and try to learn the other person's language.

But when you and a loved one don't use the same love styles, you usually *don't* know it. So you're *trying* to communicate, but not succeeding.

Six styles of loving

Every one of us gives and receives love in one or more preferred styles. Most often, a person gives and receives love in the same style or styles, but that's not always true. Sometimes a person has learned not to express love in a style they like to receive. Other individuals have learned to express their love in a style that doesn't feed their own need to receive.

If you're familiar with the book *The Five Love Languages* by Gary Chapman, you'll notice some similarities between our approaches, and also some differences. Gary talks about five "love languages," whereas in this book, I'll teach you about six "love styles." (I've put Gary's terms in parentheses next to each style name.) And while the styles do differ from each other, I'll encourage you to view them as a gentle blend, rather than completely separate with rigid boundaries. While your loved one's first and primary love style may be giving and receiving presents, he or she may also understand and appreciate body connection.

Gifts

A person with this style feels loved and appreciated when you give them presents.

If this isn't your first preferred style of giving and receiving love, but it is your loved one's, your first impression may be that she is far too materialistic. But really that isn't the case at all.

It's not the gift itself that's so important to a person with this style; it's the thought that lies behind it. These individuals may very well have grown up hearing Hallmark greeting card ads telling us, "When you care enough to give the very best." Their mantra can be shortened a bit to "When you care enough, you give."

This love style is often the primary one spoken around the holidays, especially Valentine's Day and Christmas. If this is the style you use, you may find yourself putting quite a bit of time choosing that very special present for your loved one. But how does your loved one react? Do you discover you've invested all that time and effort into your search only to receive a cursory thank-you and have the gift gently placed aside?

Consider the situation Joan found herself in one Valentine's Day. Her husband, Dale, was out of town on business. On Valentine's Day, he called before he went off to work to tell her how much he loved her. He didn't have time to buy a card, but he sent her an e-mail card. And at the end of the day he called back again to re-affirm his love. On this call, he heard his wife break down into tears. "You don't love me," she sniffled. "You don't love me." Thinking he had been a conscientious and good husband, calling twice and sending an email, Dale was baffled at this seemingly random and unnecessary outburst.

"If you truly loved me," she sobbed, "you would have sent me flowers or chocolate or something. I stayed home all day waiting for a gift to arrive!"

Dale had *expressed* his love, but in a style that meant Joan couldn't *receive* it.

I have a young niece whose primary style is Gifts. Every time she visits me, she asks, "Do have any presents for me, Auntie?" To be honest, it took me some time to realize that is how she perceives a good relationship: through the giving of gifts. The corollary to this, of course, is that she's excellent at *giving* gifts to those who mean a lot to her life.

You'll find as you start to notice love styles more that people are usually best at expressing love in the style or styles they prefer to receive.

Body Connection

Craig and Jennifer were taking a stroll together in the community park near their home. As they walked, they came upon a couple who were probably in their 70s or beyond walking in front of them. They were lovingly holding hands.

Touched, Craig reached for Jennifer's hand. She pulled back. He quickly found himself defending his action. "The couple ahead looked so much in love," he said, "even when you look at them from behind. I just thought that was awesome and we could do the same."

"You know I love you, Craig," she said. Her voice softened. "But I don't need to hold your hand when we walk to tell you that. You already know it."

For Craig, that body connection, the very act of touching the one he loved, even in small ways, was important to him. It was his way of showing Jennifer how much he loved her. He's not alone in using this style. Research is now confirming that skin-to-skin contact is the most basic form of human nurturing, and this is true not just for lovers or married couples.

Touch is fundamental to our very survival since birth. It has been shown that infants who don't receive an adequate amount of physical contact actually are at a higher risk for developing behavioral, emotional, and social problems as they grow. Research reveals that infants can grow ill and even die without human contact.

Those who use the style of touch feel loved (and express love) through some form of physical contact. This body connection need not be extravagant. I remember my father rising from the kitchen table after dinner every single evening, merely touching my mom on the shoulder as he passed her. It took me years to be able to interpret this as a "thank you" and "I love you."

When someone like Craig has their touch rejected, they are likely to feel unloved, and less close to the person who doesn't want their touch.

Practical Assistance

When you help out with washing the dishes, taking out the garbage, or any other form of assistance, you may very well be letting your loved one know how much you love him or her. For those who use the love style of practical assistance, the need to feel loved stems from being a part of an interconnected group. They want to be shown love through thoughtful daily acts.

Melissa couldn't understand why her husband, Joe, never offered to do little things around the house. She felt like she was nagging even for him to take his own dinner plate to the kitchen counter. "Doesn't he realize that I work too?" she lamented to a friend over coffee one day. "Do you know how much it would mean to me if he did even the smallest things? I'm beginning to think he doesn't love me!"

For individuals who need practical help to be reassured of love, even the smallest effort represents an affirmation of your bond with them. And people who offer or perform acts of service are *demonstrating* they care. These may very well be the first individuals within your group that you turn to for assistance, because they've offered it so often in the past and have stood with you so many times before.

These are also the people most likely to be hurt if you *don't* offer practical help, or say you'll help and fail to deliver. To someone with the Practical Assistance love style, failure to help means you don't really care about them.

The most effective way to tell these individuals "I love you" is to say "Allow me to do that for you," and then follow through and do it.

Meaningful Time

What exactly is "meaningful time?" In a nutshell, it's any time spent with your loved one that *they* find meaningful.

The key to experiencing successful meaningful time isn't so much the *amount* of time you spend with the individual, but the awareness that you're there together, giving each other undivided attention.

The husband in one couple I know had a long commute to Philadelphia. Each workday, he rose at 4:30 in the morning, and left the house by 5:30 or 5:45 AM. His wife also got up at 4:30 so they could spend time together. For them, that time spent sitting and drinking coffee and discussing the morning news was meaningful. Both were fully present, without the distraction of housework, the needs of their child, or the phone ringing. (Who in their right mind would call at that hour?) It was, in a very real sense "their time." Both of them understood this without ever having to explain it to each other. Here is an example of how things can work when both partners in a relationship use the same love style.

Children who beg you to play house, hide and seek, or any other games with them may relate primarily via Meaningful Time. If you join them wholeheartedly, they'll feel loved. But if you are distracted, impatient, or try to quickly end the game, they're likely to feel less loved and needier. It's like giving a chilly person a drafty blanket full of holes. Again, the *amount* of time isn't as significant as the fact that you're fully absorbed *being with them.*

Words of Love and Support

Some individuals really do need to hear you speak your love. A song from 1966 said "Words of love so soft and tender won't win a girl's heart anymore." Well, that's not quite right. Many women love to hear those sweet nothings whispered in their ears, and so do many men.

Scientists tell us that the average individual uses three of their senses the most when they observe and evaluate life around them: sight, sound, and touch. And just as some people love Body Connection, others speak the language of... well... language. Hearing "I love you" is very important to them.

My best friend in high school would occasionally spend the night at my house. Every time she called home, she ended her call to her mother by saying, "I love you." My family never did that. In fact, at the time I thought it was a silly, even useless waste of time to tell a family member that you love them. Of course you do! Doesn't everyone understand that? Doesn't everyone know it automatically? (Of course, I never told my friend this!)

Later I acquired a spouse and a family of my own. My spouse, who was working out of town called me at work. I ended the call with "I love you." The response of my office workers was immediate and loud. "We love you too, honey!" they practically shouted in unison. I knew they meant it, and I was astounded how great it made me feel. In the intervening years from high school to adulthood, Words of Love and Support had become extremely important to me.

This experience taught me that love styles can change. Perhaps it was the death of my parents that created this need — waking up one morning realizing I never verbalized how much I loved them, and that my chance was gone.

Perhaps it was the very real feeling of my own mortality once my child was born.

Whatever the cause of my shift in the use of love style, it became a need, not only for me but for my spouse as well. And it served us well. Today, I end calls with my daughter who lives in another state with a simple statement of my love. I also make sure I tell her how proud I am of her, and how much I appreciate her in my life. I even text her that I love her. Is this her primary love style? To be honest, I'm not sure, but she knows that it's important to me and she always responds in kind.

Sincerity is the key to making words of love and appreciation meaningful in your life and in the life of your loved one. If you say "I love you" like you were reading from a cue card, or tell someone "Your great!" in a flat, bored, or angry voice, it just won't work. Express positive feelings and praise *that you really mean,* and your loved ones are much more likely to respond well — and know you love them.

Deep Listening

Most people deeply desire to be seen, heard and understood. For some people this is more important than almost anything else. If your loved one's love style is Deep Listening, the best thing to do for them is listen.

Listening is more difficult than it seems. We come into a conversation with our own wants, desires, and histories. If you are "listening" but really thinking about what you are going to say when your loved one finishes speaking, they are probably not going to feel deeply heard.

It takes some focus to not listen to someone else from our own perspective. That's the difference between normal listening and Deep Listening.

For your loved one who uses the love style of Deep Listening, he or she wants to know you are fully listening with your heart. When you listen deeply, the other person can feel it. When I have a heart-to-heart with my best friend, I know that she is not only listening to me, but hearing every word I say, and feeling all my emotions too. I feel safe talking to her, because I can feel her love for me, and I feel really, deeply, heard.

There is a connection that you can feel — almost like a "click" — when you are listening deeply to someone, and completely get what they are saying. You can both feel love flow between you. It is a lovely moment when that happens, and I bet that if this is your loved one's love style, this book will help you have those moments again and again!

Remember, the goal with all of the love styles is to express love in whatever ways have the highest impact and make the biggest difference for your loved ones!

You're going to discover exactly *how* you can do that in the next six chapters.

CHAPTER 3

How to find a person's love style

First, let's find *your* love style. Going through the process yourself will teach you a lot about how to find other people's love styles.

What is your primary love style?

Below are three methods to discover your primary love style.

How do you like to give love?

Take a good look at how you like to *give* love. Is it through words? Actions? Gifts? Touch? Spending time with your loved one? Listening? Most people naturally give *and* receive love most strongly in the same style.

How do you like to receive love?

Now think about how you like to *receive* love. Remember a time when you felt really loved and appreciated. Now remember a second time, and a third. That's three times when you felt loved and appreciated.

What is *similar* about those situations? Did you notice that you felt loved when:

- ♥ The person gave you thoughtful gifts?

- ♥ They touched you, held you, kissed you, or offered you physical contact?

- ♥ They helped you with something — taking the time to assist with a chore or a project?

- ♥ They told you they love you, or appreciated or supported you verbally?

- ♥ You spent meaningful one-on-one time together?

- ♥ They let you talk, and you felt deeply listened to.

I asked you to find three times you felt really loved because you may have *multiple* love styles that make you feel loved. When you look at several situations, you can notice similarities. You will probably find that one love style really makes the most difference for you.

Evaluate your relationships

Another more in-depth way to consider it is to ask the following questions of yourself. (You can also use these with a loved one to help discover their love style.)

♥ What do you desire more of in your relationships? Is there anything that is particularly lacking (touch, assistance, gifts, loving words, "really" spending time together, feeling heard)?

♥ If you could ask one thing of your loved one, what would it be? What do you request most often?

♥ What does your loved one do or say (or *not* do or say) that hurts you most deeply? The opposite of what hurts you is probably your strongest love style. For instance, a Body Connection person may find lack of touch or hostile touch especially hard to deal with.

♥ How do you express your love? Do you tend to spend a lot of time buying gifts (big or little)? Are you a toucher? Do you tell people how much they mean to you? Organize outings or situations where you can spend one-on-one time with someone? Listen to people? Help them out? The way you give is often the way you like to receive.

♥ How do you *not* give love? What are some of the things that the person you are in a relationship with tells you that they wished you did more of? When you look at the different styles of love, which one seems the most foreign, or maybe beneath you?

Sometimes figuring out your strongest love style or styles can be tricky. One of my clients never gave words of love and support because when she was a child she was rejected for doing so. But after she answered the quick quiz and in-depth questions, we realized that having a partner who gave her words of love and support, and who encouraged her to speak in return, was exactly what she longed for most in a relationship!

So finding your love style can be a little wiggly. Nevertheless, if you spend 15 minutes really thinking about situations where you felt loved or unloved, you'll start to see a pattern. I've worked with many clients who felt unsure of what their love styles were, which became very clear after doing this exercise.

What is their love style?

To find someone else's primary love style without asking them, you can go through the exercises above and answer the questions as if you were the other person. Ask yourself what that person requests of you. What types of giving and receiving has she or he especially enjoyed? How does he or she express his or her love to you?

You can also just ask the other person "How do you know you are loved?" and notice how they answer!

If the person is willing, you can take them through the exercises that you did above to figure out *your* love style.

Another option is to offer the other person a choice. "Would you rather have a back rub, or for me to do the laundry? Would you rather me buy you a gift for Valentine's Day, or that I take time off work and go for a long walk with you?"

These questions can be great conversation starters! They can help you understand each other better, talk through and heal past wounds, and learn how to give in the love style or styles that each of you needs.

Confusion and Resistance

Many people find they have resistance to giving (or getting!) love in a particular love style. Sometimes the *style* is okay, but a particular *expression* is not. For instance, my client John felt okay with expressing Words of Love and Support, but had huge resistance to saying "I love you" even to his wife and children.

When my clients have trouble understanding, giving, or receiving in a particular love style, I suggest doing some homework:

Think about the love style you just don't get, or have resistance to giving or receiving. Are there childhood memories associated with it? Did your parents tell you that it wasn't necessary to say what you felt? Did you give a present to a friend who didn't like it, and made you feel bad? Were you not allowed to hug the people you loved? I bet that something related to the love style you are least foreign in will come up. Many people find that simply knowing where their difficulty with a love style comes from makes it much easier to give in that style, especially with practice.

If you're reluctant to express love in a particular way, especially if you had bad experiences with that person or love style before, I recommend finding someone you're *not* so close to, or an encouraging friend you really trust, and doing one or more practice sessions. Give love in that style, and have your friend accept it and give you positive feedback in *your* love style. Once you're more comfortable giving love that way, you can move up to expressing love with the easier people in your life who use that style. Clients of mine who had a particularly rocky relationship with a spouse or partner often find that practicing first with a friend helps them get comfortable enough with their partner's love style to give it successfully.

Sometimes people have trouble receiving in their preferred love style — usually because of bad past experiences or being told that was the "wrong" way to receive love. Again, practice with a loving friend until you get comfortable can really help.

Giving from the love styles

Now that you have a sense of the love styles, the next step is to have really practical ways to give from them.

If you are a Body Connection person, you probably know how to touch people. Maybe you've studied massage and are excellent at that love style.

When you find out your loved one feels really loved when they get words of love and support, what do you do? You use this book to figure out how to express love in ways that work for them!

The next six chapters explore each love style in depth. Whatever your loved one's love style or styles, you'll learn practical ways to fill their "love tank" and help them feel loved, wanted, and cherished.

I strongly suggest that you read all six chapters. If your primary concern is a particular relationship, go ahead and read the relevant chapter first. Then read the other chapters. *Love styles affect all your significant relationships.* Whether you're dealing with a partner, spouse, child, parent, friend, or someone at work, having the ability to help the other person feel valued and appreciated will do wonders to make that relationship better.

This book is a guide to help you find ways to express love, affection, and appreciation based on the other person's love style. I am very confident that after reading this book, you will be able to express love and appreciation effectively to anyone whose love style you can figure out.

The one thing you MUST do to make love styles work

As you read the rest of this book, learning exactly how to give to loved ones in their love styles, keep one vital factor in mind: **Engagement is crucial!** None of these styles is worth anything if you do them mechanically or don't fully participate. It's very important that you stay in the present moment – the here and now – when expressing love and appreciation.

If you're telling your mate how he or she means so much to you, and using their preferred love style of Words of Love and Support, but you're creating tomorrow's "to do" list for work or checking your phone for a text message from a friend, then *your actions undermine your words*. And trust me, your mate will notice! Rather than feeling loved and cherished by your words, it's more likely they'll feel you're neglecting them, don't care, or don't really mean what you say.

In fact, *insincerely* using someone's love style may be worse than not expressing love at all! That's because as someone receives *loving* messages most strongly in a particular style, they also receive *unloving* messages using the same style!

Someone whose love style is Words will be most hurt by "loving" words you don't mean. Someone whose main style is Gifts will be most hurt by an insincere, inappropriate, or thoughtless gift.

When you spend time with a loved one, *focus on them.* You might even imagine that for your special time together, they are the only other person in the world. Love expressed from that deep focus is love they're most likely to receive and feel.

Come with me as we learn more about the six styles of love, how to interpret them in your relationships, and how to use them to transform the very fabric of your life!

CHAPTER 4

Gifts

Giving presents is the most classic type of gift giving. We give gifts on Christmas and Valentine's Day. Sometimes we put a lot of effort into them, and sometimes we don't.

If your loved one feels loved when they get gifts, then they will ask for them — either verbally or non-verbally. Sometimes this is a challenge for people who use other love styles. They feel that the people who get and receive love through Gifts are overly materialistic. When we start to see that as a judgment, we can start to see through it and into the truth that if we want to show our love to these people, gifts are the way to go.

One way to look at it is that what you are giving to your loved one is energy. That energy may be delivered in words, listening, spending time with them, physical touch, in doing labor directly for them, or in doing work for someone else (for example, your clients or boss), and converting the money you make into a gift for them.

Types of gifts

The first rule of giving gifts is that they should be from the heart. You should really hold your loved one in your mind when selecting the present.

I've discovered that while there are many types of gifts that people like to be given, They seem to naturally fall into four major categories:

1. **Expensive gifts.** These people want to know that you are willing to spend money on them. It shows them that you love them so much that you would buy them something expensive. These people feel great when you get them something valuable — something that they want or have always wanted.

2. **Small, numerous gifts.** If your loved one is this type of gift lover, then they like to get many smaller gifts. These gifts need not be expensive, just tokens that you are thinking of them. Often this is the lover who is happy when you bring her flowers every week, or bring him a special snack on your way home from work on a regular basis. The trick here

is to make a clear decision about whether you want to be predictable or not. She may feel comforted and loved if you bring her flowers every Thursday. But then you are in trouble if you forget. Or you can choose to bring gifts sporadically, bring him several small gifts one week, then only one gift the next. Of course, the best thing to do is to communicate about it and find a giving style that works for both of you.

3. **Handmade gifts.**   Handmade gifts are a labor of love. They share a little bit of you with your loved one and show him or her a special type of love. Some people really appreciate it when you manifest your love in something hand-made, while others don't really care.

4. **All gifts.**   Some people like a mixture of all gift types.

How to find the right kind of gift for your loved one

How do you know which kind of gift is the right one for your loved one?

The simplest way is to ask. Ask your loved one what their favorite gifts were. Then ask a second and more important question: "What made that gift so special?" You might find from this that there are special circumstances or words that go with giving gifts that they particularly need.

The second way is trying things. See what really lights them up. If you give them a big gift that they can show all their friends and touch every day, do they love it? Try a couple of smaller gifts and see if you get a similar or better reaction. What if you give them a handmade gift?

You also need to consider your budget and your style.

Consider it all with an air of experimentation. Once you suspect that your loved one has the love style of Gifts, you probably do better with him or her already. Now refine that so you can get the maximum love juice for the minimum effort.

Choosing the perfect gift

There are so many different gifts to give. When you give a gift, you are telling the person you care about something specific, using their love style. What do you want him or her to hear? The following list shows some of the specific messages you can share by gift giving.

♥ **Gifts that say "I listen."**   Listen to your loved one. What do they *say* they want? One of my clients tried this out, and in one day heard his partner lamenting about needing a new stapler and a specific pair of boots. He went out and bought them for her, and she really felt loved! People who love gifts will often tell you what they like. Go to the mall with them, notice what they seem to particularly love and then go back, pick it up, wrap it, and give it to them.

♥ **Gifts that share about you.**   Your loved ones, especially your partner, wants to feel close to you. Many people with the Gifts love style appreciate gifts that show more about who *you* are and what you share with them. If you've been spending a lot of time taking photos with your camera, why not get one or two printed and framed, and give your loved one the gift of literally seeing the world through your eyes?

♥ **Gifts for adventures together.**   If you are planning a trip or adventure, you can give gifts that relate to that — for example a new video camera for a vacation, or a new frying pan for that cooking class you are taking together.

♥ **Random gifts.**   Some people like completely random gifts — an interesting book that you find by chance, a cool-looking pair of earrings, a fun pen. These are generally small, fun gifts.

♥ **Fun surprises,**   such as a special dinner, treat, or that gadget your loved one has been drooling over for months.

♥ **Gifts related to their passions.** If you know your loved one is very excited about golf, you can search on the internet for "golf gifts" or "gifts for golfers." The same is true of most hobbies.

♥ **Non-physical gifts.** Sometimes the best gift is nonphysical: a donation to their favorite charity, a balloon ride, a vacation, or a ticket to a concert or play. These can still be gifts, and you can even wrap the ticket or receipt in a card or a book about the subject.

♥ **Gifts that they request.** A great way to put together a list of gifts is to ask them what they want. Write it down. Give it to them!

Things to remember when giving gifts

There are four important things to remember when giving gifts to your loved one.

1. **Give in love and appreciation.** The most important thing to remember in giving gifts is that you are giving because you love the other person. If you give a present with a feeling of resentment or obligation, your loved one will feel it. Humans are extremely good at picking up non-verbal cues, so make sure that when you give him that expensive golf bag he requested, you are feeling the love, and

even say it: "Honey, I wanted to give this to you to show you how much I love you."

2. **Experiment.** Try different ways of giving gifts, different cards, different settings, different things that you say to your loved one when you give them a gift. See how they respond. Learn from this and find the best combination of what makes your loved one feel loved, and what you feel good about giving.

3. **Wrap it.** Always wrap a gift unless your loved one says they don't want it wrapped. Even then, wrap it sometimes just to test their reaction. A wrapped gift might get a better response! For many people with the Gifts love style, the wrapping is part of the fun, lets them know you care enough about their pleasure to bother with the extra work, or both.

4. **Keep the receipt,** especially if the gift is expensive. The guy in the story above who gave his partner new boots? She had to return them 3 times to get ones that fit! Especially if the gift is more expensive, keep the receipt and be open to making an exchange and learning more about what your loved one loves.

By using your loved one's love style, giving the right kind of gifts, and following the tips in this section, you will very clearly show them how much you love them *in a way that they understand and find satisfying.* This is bound to improve your relationship, and it can be a lot of fun for both of you, too.

If your love style is Gifts

In our culture, we get mixed messages about giving and receiving gifts. On one hand, we give gifts to show our love for birthdays, Christmas, and Valentine's Day. On the other hand, someone who likes getting a lot of gifts can be seen as overly materialistic.

So, what if you love gifts? What if getting gifts is what lets you know that someone loves you?

Accept and revel in it!

Lots of people are like you. Being you is just fine. Once you teach your loved ones *what* and *when* to give, the Gifts love style can be one of the easier ones for your loved ones to accommodate.

Don't expect others to read your mind

There is a widespread myth that if someone loves you, they will "just know" what to give you and how to give it. Wrong! Your loved ones are not mind readers. You need to let them know what you want so they can please you.

Another myth is the idea that a gift "doesn't count" if you have to ask for it. Nope. Your loved ones might be able to give exactly what you want without you asking *after* you coach them... but it's almost certain they *won't* get everything right until you do. And even then, you can often help them love you by telling them exactly what you want. If they know what you want and can deliver, and it makes you happy, everybody wins!

Learn to communicate what you like

How do you do this?

Share this book with your loved one. Figure out together what your love styles are. Make a list of ways you can satisfy each other. When you do this it can become quite clear that it's an exchange of love. Maybe they like back rubs, or for you to make them dinner, and you like flowers. Both of you want gifts; it's just that they want actions and you want objects.

Some people who have more money than time will be overjoyed that they can buy you something nice (especially if you give them a list), because while they love you madly, they don't feel like they have the time for some of the more time-intensive love styles.

Give positive feedback. Research shows that this works really well. When they give you something you like, light up! Let them know how much it means to you when they buy you gifts.

If your loved one gives you something that *isn't* what you want, it's important to give feedback in a way that encourages rather than discourages them. If they feel criticized or punished, they may just give up and stop trying! Make a big deal of the real effort they made to please you. Then you might say to them something like, "I really appreciate you doing this to please me. I would love it even more if you gave me _____."

Talk about it.   Your loved ones want to make you happy and to show their love, so make it easy for them! Tell them what you like; you can even make a list. Look through the ideas above and if you're not sure what you like best, give your loved ones a chance to try several of them!

CHAPTER 5

Body Connection

If your loved one craves a body connection, the best way you can give it to them is to touch them. This is one of the easiest love styles, yet sometimes the most challenging.

Body connection doesn't have to mean sex. Body connection can be as simple as holding someone's hand, stroking their hair, or touching their shoulder when you speak. It's also possible to create a deep Body Connection without touch; something as simple like breathing together or gazing into each other's eyes.

Sometimes the only loving your loved one needs is the simple touch that you might not think is that important! For them, touch is the best way for you to communicate your love in a way they understand.

What is Body Connection?

Of course, it's physically easy to touch your loved ones. The difference between a simple touch and creating a body connection is *the way it feels to both parties.* Body connection *feels good.* Whether you're physically touching or not, you and your loved one are in physical rapport and in sync with each other.

If you are touching your loved one and you don't feel good about it, then your loved one will pick up on that, and *they* probably won't feel so good. You're touching, but not connected.

Body connection while you are doing something else *may* work, depending on what you are doing and what kind of connection the two of you have. If you and your loved one have an emotionally deep conversation while holding hands or gazing into each other's eyes, or you cuddle while watching a movie and enjoying each other's presence, the connection between your bodies *adds* to the experience. On the other hand, even if you and your mate are wrapped in a passionate embrace, if one or both of you feel angry or resentful, or you're distracted thinking or worrying about something else, the connection between your bodies *conflicts with* your emotions and experience, which probably *won't* work.

I have found that many people are so touch-starved that *any* touch feels good, at least to begin with. When one or both people emotionally disconnect, at first it may not be clear to either person that something is "off" or wrong.

When body connection works, it can create a sense of connection that seems profound, often magical or spiritual.

Touching well is a skill

Many couples who love each other are mismatched when it comes to touch.

When I notice that a couple has significantly different desires concerning touch, I generally start working with them around it by talking about it. Sometimes there is an event in one partner's history that makes that person uncomfortable with touch. In might be abuse, experience with a previous partner who rejected touch, or just growing up in a family that didn't touch each other much. Sometimes one or both people need to *learn* to create a body connection, just as we needed to learn to walk and drive.

This idea may seem strange to someone who loves touch, but as with many aspects of relationships, *touching well is a learned skill.* The type of touch that feels good for one person is not necessarily the same for the other. Most people assume that "pleasant touch" is what they themselves like; and this can cause real problems in a relationship.

In one couple I worked with, she *hated* light touch because she found it ticklish and uncomfortable. Yet that was her partner's favorite way to be touched! The firm touch she liked felt too heavy to him, and wasn't erotic. As you might imagine, they had sexual problems until they realized that each of them needed to touch the other in the way the *recipient* liked to receive.

Learn to touch skillfully

It is up to you to learn how to touch your loved one skillfully by finding ways to touch that work *for them.*

How do you do that? Here are some easy techniques I have taught to clients with great success. These work with lovers and spouses, children, relatives, and friends.

I've also had clients tell me they successfully used some of these methods in the workplace to smooth a troublesome relationship or help someone on their team feel more valued. Unfortunately touch can be a tricky thing in a business setting, so make *sure* that your touch can't be misinterpreted as sexual — either by the recipient, or by others.

Ask for feedback

One of the easiest ways to learn your loved one's touch preferences is to simply ask them for feedback. Here are some simple methods:

- Ask them how and when they like to be touched, and how and when they don't.

- Touch them, and ask, "How does this feel?"

Ask for examples

This is an especially good approach if there are touch or connection problems between you and your loved one. Ask

- "When I touch you in ways you really like, what am I doing?"

- "What about that works for you?"

- "When I touch you in ways you *don't* like, what am I doing?"

- "What about that doesn't work for you?"

Their answers may surprise you. Sometimes the touch that one person does casually without paying a lot of attention is what matters most to their loved one! Or you may discover that a type of connection you've struggled to give them is something they don't really care about.

Their answer will also tell you more about how they experience touch, which will help you figure out better ways to connect with them.

Have them touch you

Ask the other person to touch *you* in the ways *they* want to be touched. Now do your best to duplicate what they're doing by touching them. Ask them for feedback: "Is that what you want?" Keep following what they do until you're able to touch them the way they like.

Try things and notice the responses

If you've been touching your loved one on the shoulder, try giving them a hug. If you've been cuddling, try holding hands. Notice what they respond well to, and do more of it.

Do keep checking in with them verbally, especially if you're doing this exercise with your lover or spouse. A lot of people respond more strongly to sensations they *don't* like than to things they *do* like. If you just chase the strongest responses, you could end up doing something they really *dislike*.

Practice being present in the moment

Whereas the previous exercises focused on your loved one and what *they* like, this one addresses *your* inner experience.

You might think "What does my inner experience have to do with anything? I'm just touching them!" Well, people are surprisingly skilled at picking up very subtle nonverbal signals. That's even more true for people who use Body Connection as their preferred love style. If you're not present, they may feel something is weird or not right.

Being present also makes a stronger connection possible *for you.* I have found that this exercise is especially useful for people who tend to be distracted or not present in their bodies when they are with their loved ones.

As a fringe benefit, a lot of these clients also report that as they become more present, their romantic partner says they are a better lover.

You and your loved one can do this exercise with each other at the same time. Or you can do it when you are with them and doing something other activity, such as cuddling or watching TV. Here's how:

1. At a time when you feel relaxed, take a few deep breaths, all the way into your belly, and really notice how you feel.

2. Remember a time when you felt really happy and relaxed and completely in your body.

3. Now reach out and touch your loved one somewhere that feels comfortable for you.

4. Notice what it is like to really be present in your body, and in connection with them.

5. Hold this body connection as long as it feels comfortable. If it feels good, start to stoke them and see how they respond. If that sense of body connection

slips away, that's fine. Just remember what it felt like and move towards it in your interactions.

Body Connection ideas

If you find that your loved one receives love through Body Connection, here are some ways to demonstrate your love. Some of these will work with anyone. Others are more suited to a lover or spouse.

Hold their hand. This type of touch works in virtually any situation to let your loved one know that you care. It's great for connecting with children, grandparents, friends, and of course your spouse or lover.

The down side of holding hands is that if you're doing something else at the same time, it's easy to get distracted. Or worse, impatient or angry, which could really send the wrong message! So be mindful. With intention and presence, holding hands can be a beautiful way to connect.

Give them a big hug. This is something you can do every day, perhaps when they or you get home, or when you feel particularly close.

The important thing here is to *stop the other things you're doing,* mentally and physically, and really be present with them while you hug them.

Before you hug, take a deep breath, and really get present in your body. Now give your loved one a full-body hug. Ideally, your bodies should touch from thigh to shoulder. This creates a much stronger Body Connection than the "A-frame" hug where only arms and upper chest touch. If you're hugging a child, kneel to bring yourself to their level.

Rather than squashing your loved one, hold them in a way they'll find comfortable. And while you are in the hug really notice how you feel, and remember how much you care for and appreciate them.

A big hug can last anywhere from 20 seconds to 2 minutes. I promise: if your partner, child, or close friend loves Body Connection, giving them a big hug every day will have a wonderful impact on your relationship!

Comfort with touch. When your loved one who prefers Body Connection gets upset, touch is the best way to comfort them. One couple I worked with felt distant from each other. They soon realized that by giving each other comforting touch instead of trying to comfort each other with words, they could really *feel* each other's love.

Next time your loved one seems upset, try this: While facing them and making eye contact, rub their arms and shoulders soothingly. This is not a massage, and not about sensuality — you are comforting them. You can also hold your loved one. See how your loved one reacts — if he or she seems to relax a bit, continue with this comforting touch.

Offer them a massage. This makes a great gift for a body connection person. Depending on your relationship and comfort level, this can be anything from massaging their hands or feet, to giving them a full-body massage or even an erotic massage. If you like Gifts, give them a coupon good for a 20 minute massage from you. This will please you both.

Take them dancing. You don't have to know how to dance — just go out somewhere that has music you can move to together. With a spouse or lover, you can stay home, put on some of your favorite music, and slow dance. It's a wonderful way to create that body connection, and enjoy being close and comfortable while touching.

Take a touch-oriented class together. Find one you both think you'll enjoy, and take it together. It could be a partner dance class, a massage class, or anything that involves you touching each other. It's important that you take the class with your loved one, as they want to feel love *from you.*

Breathe together. This is an exercise I give to almost all my clients who are couples. Set a timer for a few minutes — perhaps start with 2 minutes and work up to 5. Put your right hand over their heart, look into their eyes, take deep breaths, and match your breathing to theirs. When they breathe in, you breathe in. When they exhale, you exhale. If you get uncomfortable with the eye contact, close your eyes for a moment. Once you feel comfortable, really think about how much you love them while you look into their eyes.

Express your passion.   Many of my couples clients find this is a great way to recharge their connection to each other. Use a combination of touch, loving looks, and loving words to demonstrate how much you care. Here's one way to do it:

Sit and face each other, and make eye contact. With your hand, touch your loved one, starting with their face. Stroke their face gently, and tell them how much you love them. Let them see it in your eyes! You can then move to touching their chest or hands. You are letting your loved one really know, through touch and your words and the look in your eye, how passionate you are about them.

Create a pleasure map.   This is a great way to explore a spouse or lover's pleasure zones, and find sensitive spots even they may not have known about.

Start by talking about boundaries — where they are comfortable being touched, and any off-limits zones. Have them lie down wearing as few clothes as you both feel comfortable with. Now take your time exploring their body with your hands — and perhaps your nails, lips, tongue, and whatever else you might have that feels interesting (feathers seem like a good idea). Vary the firmness of your touch from light stroking to deep massage. Especially sensitive areas usually include creases (behind the knees, along the toes, the buttocks crease, elbows) and typical erogenous zones (nipples, genitals, ears, neck). Also explore other areas such as the backs of the legs, nape of the neck, small of the back, and ankles.

This exercise can be done over and over. You learn what pleasures your partner while you give them intense pleasure.

Create an evening of sensual pleasure. This is a great way for lovers or spouses to connect. Pick a time when you can set aside an evening with no distractions. Let it be just for the two of you, your own evening of connection.

Setting the mood is important. Light candles, dim the lights, play soft music. Let your partner know that this evening is about their sensual pleasure! Let them relax in their favorite chair, couch, or on the bed. Feed them their favorite food, give them a nice massage (maybe now that you've taken a massage class together), and let them know how much you love making them feel good. This is the time to be fully present with your loved one. By being in the now together, you can let your pleasure soar to new heights!

If your love style is Body Connection

If you love to feel your loved one touch you, and it makes you feel really loved, let them know! How?

Well, the easiest way is to tell them! "I really love it

when we are in physical contact" works. Or you can say something a little more romantic, like "I love it when you touch me — it makes me feel so good inside." Many people are waiting and hope for permission to touch. Give it!

If your loved one is less of a toucher, or gets bothered by touch, find a way to touch that feels safe for both of you. You might start with a foot or hand massage, or by holding hands or combing each other's hair.

Make sure you avoid behaviors that will discourage your loved one from touching you. For instance, if they touch you in a way you don't like, and you pull away or say "Not like that!", they are likely to assume you don't want to be touched *at all*. A much better approach is to say, "Mm. I'd like that even better if you _____." Then describe what you want.

Encourage your loved one when they touch you. Lean into the touch, smile, say "Mm!" or "That feels good." Remember, your loved one with another love style may not have the strong intuition about touch that lets you know when someone likes being touched. When you like what someone does, make it obvious to them so they know to do more of it.

Non-sexual touch

In US culture, it is sometimes seen as inappropriate to get touch from people of the same gender, or from people who we are not in a romantic relationship with. This can be a challenge for the Body Connection love style.

Some of my clients have used the following ways to get the touch they desperately needed:

- Taking a partner dance class (like waltz or tango).

- Taking a massage class or becoming a masseuse.

- Taking up a physical sport, like wrestling or rugby.

Another tactic you can use to increase the touch in your life is to do touch testing. This is where you consciously touch the people in your life – generally starting with the shoulder or elbow. You might touch them in talking to them, or in passing. Then watch for their reaction. If they smile or move towards you, you can continue to touch them this way, and maybe increase touch.

Be careful though that your touches don't get misconstrued as romantic. A good way to stay safe is to stick to the elbow or shoulder, and if you want more touch, to talk about it.

Finally, really enjoy your hugs. One of my clients hugs until he feels the subtle signals that the other person wants to stop. He's never the one to finish a hug; although he releases people as soon as he feels the first sign that they are done with the hug. I met him at a social function one time and saw him give another guest a 10 minute hug! Maybe they were both testing this idea.

CHAPTER 6

Practical Assistance

Helping someone is a great way to show you care. Think about it: Helping takes your effort, time and skill. And it all goes to the special someone you help out: Your mate, your child, your friend, your mother.

A couple of weeks ago I overheard the neighborhood kids as they were working on a bike.

"Thanks for helping me fix my bike!" the first one said.

"That's what friends are for," the second responded.

"Yeah! That's friendship," the first replied.

What is Practical Assistance?

Practical Assistance is helping someone with a task, especially one that they don't want to do. Many people who don't use this love style do not understand how loving it can feel to get help.

Our ancestors lived in tightly knit communities where helping each other was a basic survival trait. Communities that cooperated survived, while those that did not cooperate perished. Helping someone with their tasks or chores is a fundamentally nurturing act, one that can show that you care on a deep level.

Practical Assistance differs from Meaningful Time in that you don't need to be with your loved one for them to feel loved. If they urgently need an errand run across town, they'll feel loved when you do it for them.

Assistance must be something that actually helps

I worked with a couple named Chad and Susan. Chad loved banana bread, and Susan loved dark chocolate bars. Because of the way they had grown up, Chad equated home-made banana bread with love, while Susan equated dark Belgian chocolate with love.

So Chad was feeling down, what did Susan do? She gave him love – dark Belgian chocolate. Since Chad didn't really like chocolate, this didn't make him feel loved at all! Because she didn't give him what *he* needed, Chad felt like Susan wasn't supporting him, and felt even worse.

Susan saw his pain and, knowing that love meant dark Belgian chocolate, bought him more and presented it with love and care. Chad, longing for the smell of home-made banana bread, but feeling too down to ask for it, just felt worse.

When they came to me they were both miserable. Susan was doing everything she could to give Chad love, and Chad just wasn't feeling loved.

With a few simple questions we were able to figure it out, and from that day on their house smelled a like banana bread!

Keeping things fair

In working with couples and families, one of the challenges that comes up repeatedly is the concept of fairness. When you love someone whose love style is Practical Assistance, you may find that you help them more than they help you. This can feel unbalanced, even unfair.

With love styles, we are not seeking equality; we are seeking balance! You want to get love expressed to you in the ways *you* prefer, and so does your loved one. If both people get that, the relationship can flourish.

If you are Body Connection person, and you love to be touched, you might assume that your partner likes to touch and be touched as well. So you may start to take their touch for granted, rather than consider it a special gift for you. Especially since touch is considered a "standard" way of showing love in a romantic relationship.

Then, when you find out that your partner is a practical assistance person, and you choose to love them in their love style, you might feel a bit resentful because you end up doing more tasks.

Three things to remember here:

1. You want to learn to notice giving and receiving in *all* love styles. Maybe your partner is making a special effort to touch you, and you don't realize that they are giving more in that arena.

2. You want to remember to give only what you feel comfortable giving. If you feel resentful, step back and reconsider. Ideally, you want to give and expect nothing in return.

3. The goal is to get both people's needs met, and sometimes that means that for a time one gives more than the other.

Let them know why you're helping

Let your Practical Assistance loved one know you are helping because you love them. This can be as simple as saying:

- "I love you and want to do something special for you, so let me iron your shirts"

- "I love you and want to show you by giving you a back rub."

- "I love you so I got you this item you want."

Knowing that you're helping because you care makes a Practical Assistance person feel loved and cared for.

Knowing what help to give

The goal with any of the love styles is to express love in whatever way has the highest impact and makes the biggest difference. People with the Practical Assistance love style like to receive assistance in various ways. Here are some ways you can figure out how they want to receive help from you.

Just help

An easy thing to start with is to just help out. Maybe your loved one is doing dishes, or laundry, or gardening. Offer to help and notice how they react. If they decline your offer, then notice if they are doing it to be polite ("No, I couldn't ask that of you") or if they really enjoy doing that task ("No, I want to do this"), maybe alone ("No, I prefer gardening alone").

Often Practical Assistance people have had to "do it all themselves" or "go it alone" so much that they don't know *how* to accept help gracefully, even if they really want it. Other times you'll get a huge smile and know right away that you've found a way to show them the love you feel.

Ask them what you can do to help

Another way to offer practical assistance is to ask. "Honey, I love you and I'd like to help you out. What can I do to make your day easier?"

You can also ask specific things: "It looks like you have a big list of things to do today, I'd like to help. Would it be helpful if I washed the car, did the shopping or did the laundry?"

Make sure that you are offering to do things that you feel good about doing, and if your loved one says yes, do them with love!

Do what THEY value

With Practical Assistance, you demonstrate your love by doing something that your loved one wants done, not what *you* want done. If you really think it would be great if the car were washed, but they care more about having a clean kitchen, they will feel more loved when you help them with the kitchen.

Ideas for Practical Assistance

Do tasks for them. Make a list of all the tasks or chores that you both would like to get done that month, and every week or day, do one of those tasks — unasked.

Use your skills. Notice what your loved one might need that you have a special skill in and ask them if you can help them with it. If you are great at fixing things, and they have a leaky faucet, ask them if they would like you to fix it. You'll be surprised at how much that can mean to them.

Do tasks they hate. This is especially helpful if a task is something you *like* to do, or don't mind. Then both of you get to feel good!

Take on regular tasks that you know they like. If they like a clean house, and you are indifferent about it, taking the extra time to tidy up will show them you care.

Do their chores. If you usually cook and they do the dishes, offer to do the dishes every once in a while.

Here is a quick list of tasks to consider doing:

- Dishes

- Laundry
- Walking the dog
- Picking the kids up from school
- Mowing the lawn
- Making dinner
- Baking for them
- Washing their car
- Picking up dinner on the way home
- Making the bed
- Tidying the house
- Fixing something

It may be that you need to do a bit of strategizing to find out exactly the right things that make your practical assistance loved one give you that big grin. The trick is to try things, notice your loved one's reaction, and when you get a great reaction, do that thing more.

If your love style is Practical Assistance

If your love style is practical assistance, it helps to be really appreciative when your loved one does something for you. Hopefully by this time you know their love style, so use it to thank them for helping you. If they are a Body Connection person, then give them a big hug. If they are a Meaningful Time person, tell them how them helping you out will allow you to spend more time with them — then make it happen!

What you *shouldn't* do is complain, or criticize their efforts. Especially if your loved one uses the Words of Love and Support or Deep Listening love style, even a small amount of criticism or nagging can make them feel punished for trying to help you.

If they give you "help" you don't want, or give it in a way that's not what you like, you can give feedback without discouraging them by saying something like, "That's great, honey. Thank you. I'd like it even better if..." or "You know, I think I might love it if you _____")

Make sure your loved ones feel like you reward them for helping you. This will help them know how much you appreciate their help. If they feel loved and appreciated for helping you, they're much more likely to help you again. Research shows that rewards are the best way to change behavior!

CHAPTER 7

Meaningful Time

For some people, the gift of your company fills them up. If your partner has the love style of Meaningful Time, they thrive on spending time with you. To show your love, your task is to really be present with them. When you give them your undivided attention, they feel loved.

The Meaningful Time person can be a wonderful friend or partner because they love to be with you. For them, just being together can be enough. Doing chores, reading together, and interacting feels great to them.

On the minus side, if you are not a Meaningful Time person, you might feel like your loved one is a bit clingy and overly attached. Here again, it is important to remember that we're striving for a balance. What you have to give your meaningful time partner is your time! In return, they will hopefully give you what *you* need, which may be just as much of an effort for them.

What is Meaningful Time?

Meaningful Time is what's meaningful *to your loved one.* This varies a lot from person to person. One person's deeply meaningful connection time may seem superficial or boring to someone else. Possibilities include:

- Time that is shared with just the two of you.

- Time where you are focused on each other, on "being" together.

- Talking or walking together, or specific meaningful activities.

Underneath it all though, it's about stopping everything else, and really being present with your loved one. Being with them means not thinking about work, or talking on your phone, or working on the computer.

For some people meaningful time can include chores and household tasks. For others, it's one-on-one special time. You want to show your loved one that you care enough to stop everything else and focus on them.

How to express love to a Meaningful Time person

Like all of the love styles, start by figuring out the nuances of your loved one's love style. Do they like to spend time together talking? Do they prefer special activities? Do they feel nourished by spending a day together doing chores?

A great way to find out is to ask. Tell them that you really want to spend a day doing whatever they want, and see what suggestions they create.

I've found that Meaningful Time people fall into five categories, depending on what activities they find meaningful:

Deep conversation

Have you ever been so engrossed in a conversation that hours went by and you didn't notice it? This is the type of experience that the deep conversation person loves.

If your loved one feels nurtured by deep conversation, then they really want to engage with you. This is a different love style than Deep Listening because the Meaningful Time person wants your interaction. They love the engagement of talking with you, and having you respond. It's not about listening; it's about being connected. This can include anything from gossiping together to discussing philosophy, favorite interests, or life plans and goals.

How do you provide deep conversation? Here are some ideas:

- Find a book you both love and study it together. Set aside time every week to discuss what you learn from and think about the book.

- If one of you is passionate about something, or struggling with something, discuss it. One of my clients was a budding entrepreneur, and he feels extremely nurtured when he could brainstorm and engage his wife in conversation about his business. It went far beyond her listening, as she provided feedback, ideas and new points of view on the business that helped make it extremely successful.

- If you share spiritual beliefs, you can discuss them, or read various texts and discuss how they apply to your lives and the lives of those around you.

Special activities together

This type loves it when you make time to take them somewhere special — just the two of you. This could be anything from a walk in the park to a ball game or a special weekend away with no computer, cell phones, books, or kids. The trick here is to pick something you know your loved one finds special, then suggest it and make it happen. Possibilities include:

- A special dinner out with just the two of you.

- A regular get-away. One couple I know schedules one weekend get-away every 90 days just to be together.

- A surprise adventure together. This can be something they have always wanted to try, whether rock climbing, a Broadway play, or the new club in town.

Daily activities together

Some people thrive on regular company. My friend Ray and I regularly go shopping or cook dinner together. The activity is not as important as the fact that during that time we are talking and really being present with each other.

One way to create this is to have chores that you regularly do together. It might not be as efficient as doing them solo, but you'll be satisfying your loved one's deep need for company, companionship, and love.

Parallel activities together

A less common variant is people who enjoy being together while doing separate activities. For example, they like being in the same room while one of you watches a movie and the other reads a book.

Originally this would never have fit into my definition of meaningful time, as each person's focus is on something other than the other person. Over time I've learned that some people find this incredibly nurturing.

Community activities together

Some people find great joy in spending meaningful time volunteering. This can be an opportunity to be present and focused on each other while helping others.

When selecting volunteer opportunities, choose those that allow you to spend focused time together. For example, it's definitely possible to spend meaningful time together painting a homeless shelter. It's more difficult if you are staffing a book sale.

You can best express to your Meaningful Time loved one when you are with them fully, and engage in conversations and activities that you both love with your full attention. In this way, you will let them know how much you love them.

I have clients who turned their marriage around by simply scheduling a Sunday afternoon walk to their favorite bakery and back. By doing something they loved, doing it together, and having time for long and deep conversations, they showed each other how much they loved each other.

If your love style is Meaningful Time

If your love style is Meaningful Time, a few simple changes can really help connect you and your loved ones:

Ask for Meaningful Time. Many times loved ones would happily spend Meaningful Time with you; they just don't know that you need it, or how exactly to provide it. So do ask them, and be very specific about what you want. For instance, "I want to walk in the park with you, and have a real heart-to-heart conversation where we're really paying attention to each other."

Let people know when your time with them is meaningful. If your loved one doesn't share your love style, or if another *kind* of shared time is meaningful for them, they might not realize what matters most to you. So tell them!

Find things you both like to do. Because the activity is something they like, your loved one will enjoy spending the time with you, and you can get the Meaningful Time you crave.

Structure things so both your needs get met. If you can meet your need for Meaningful Time at the same time your loved one receives *their* love language, that's ideal. For instance, you might spend Meaningful Time cuddling with your loved one who likes Body Connection, or providing Deep Listening for a loved one who receives love that way. If your love styles don't work that way together, set things up so that each person gets a turn receiving in their love style.

Chapter 8

Words of Love and Support

How often do you say "I love you"? Maybe a lot, maybe a little. Some people have *never* said "I love you" to their loved ones. Some *want* to say it, but feel awkward — especially with their adult children or parents.

If your loved one has a Words of Love and Support love style, then they yearn to hear the words. They long for someone to tell them that they are appreciated, that they are doing a great job, and that they are loved.

We'll get into "I love you" later in the chapter. (Oddly enough, this can be one of the most difficult phrases to say.) Let's start with simple appreciations.

Giving praise

Here in the US, it seems like people mainly learn how to give *negative* feedback. We learn many ways to tell the people around us that we dislike what they're doing and want them to change. But we don't learn how to give praise. It's awkward. You'll find though that once you start giving people praise, they open up like a flower towards the sun.

An easy way to start is to just notice what you like about a person and tell them:

- "I like that dress, it looks great on you."
- "Thank you for doing the laundry"
- "I appreciate that you did your homework without being asked"

There's a whole body of research about the value of praise in changing people's behavior. It shows that if you praise behavior you like, and ignore behavior you don't like, you actually get more of the behavior you like. Praise has been shown to be more effective at changing behavior than negative feedback such as nagging and criticism.

Acquire the praise habit

If you don't have the praise habit, I suggest you start by giving 5 to 10 heartfelt honest compliments a day and see how the people around you change. Especially for loved ones whose primary love style is Words of Love and Support, a bit of praise can quickly make a huge improvement in your relationship!

Advanced praise techniques

Once you get the hang of giving praise, then you can start trying some advanced praise techniques. With advanced praise you give praise, then say how that affects you. For example:

- "Thank you for doing the laundry. It makes me feel grateful that you took on that task that I didn't want to do."

- "Thanks for your encouragement. It gave me the confidence to ask for a raise, and I got it!"

- "Thank you for listening to me. I feel cherished."

- "Thank you for doing your homework without being asked. It makes me feel refreshed and peaceful when things flow smoothly in the family."

Below is a list of feeling words that you can use as you start to explore how to do these more advanced praise:

- Affectionate
- Engaged
- Hopeful

- Confident
- Excited
- Grateful
- Inspired
- Joyful
- Exhilarated
- Peaceful
- Refreshed

Here is a great resource for feeling words: http://www. cnvc.org /Training/feelings-inventory

When you explain *why* you feel the way you do, it shows that you really mean the compliment that you are giving, and that you've really thought about your loved one and value them.

How to give great Words of Love and Support

Here are some tips on how to choose the proper tone and words to speak your love:

- **Be yourself.** It's the best way to speak appreciative words that are true.

- **Double-check before speaking.** If you have a compliment or affirmation in your head, double-check it before saying it out loud. Think about how these words might impact your loved one in the moment. How you would feel if someone said similar words to you? You may need to adjust *how* you say something in order to communicate the message you intend.

- **Make sure your tone matches your words.** Otherwise, your words may have an impact that's not what you intend. Is there emotion in your voice? Could the way you are saying something make it sound sarcastic, or like you are just reading a script?

- **Give the person you are speaking to time to digest what you are saying.** It is really good to pause after saying something big. Let the words wash over your loved one. Notice how they react. If there's strong emotion such as tears, a huge grin, or laughter, give them some processing time before you continue.

- **Be brave enough to take risks.** If there is something complementary or loving you have never said to your Words of Love and Support loved one, use the above tips to say it right. I see far too many people in my practice who regret not having expressed their love and appreciation to loved ones, especially when the person dies or divorces them. On the other hand, simply speaking the words that matter has turned many failing relationships around.

Public encouragement

Nothing has the potential to show your Words of Love and Support loved one how much you care about them than speaking praise in public. Public means when anyone else is around besides the two of you. If your friends, relatives, or children are there, even better! Nothing makes a mate who uses this love style glow like hearing encouragement and affirmation in the presence of others.

I had one client who never believed it when her husband told her that he loved him. We figured out that it was because he only told her when they were alone. She told him she wanted him to say it when others were around. Now, whenever they have friends or family over, he makes it a point to raise a wine glass and toast to her at dinner, sharing his love for her with everyone.

Try an experiment with your Words of Love and Support loved one. Use the same appreciative words twice – once in private and once in public. Notice how your loved one reacts. Does he or she seem more happy and deeply feeling your love in public, or in private? With this information, you can decide if public encouragement is a good fit for your loved one's love style.

Sometimes giving public praise means attending that work, school, or family event with a loved one that you would usually rather skip. But if your loved one uses this love style, this is a great opportunity to show public encouragement. By being there, and by being verbally supportive, you can really make your loved one feel great.

Written words, spoken words

Some people really need you to *say* Words of Love and Support. Unless you *speak* the words from your heart directly to them, they don't receive your gifts of love. Other people with this love style also accept written appreciation. Some ever prefer it, because they can read and enjoy your words again and again. Decades later, your loved one may still treasure that special letter or card.

When I was a child, my best friend's father would slip little notes into her lunches, so that when she was at school, she got a nice surprise. She got to read "I love you! Can't wait to see you in just a little while!" It brightened her whole day.

Here are a few suggestions for providing written Words of Love and Support to your loved one:

- Write a long list of everything you love about them (compliments and affirmations). Read it to them, and then give them the list.

- Send a quick note to them while they are at work. Email and text messages are a blessing to people with this love style.

- Write out the story of your lives together, and read it together at a special time, such as before bed.

- Sit with your kids and write down what they say about your spouse or partner in response to, "Mom/dad is wonderful because _____." Then give this to him or her.

- Print out a favorite photograph of the two of you. Using a permanent marker or paint pen, write "I love you!" on the front.

- Make a video recording of you saying what you love about your loved one, your home, the work that they do, etc. (This is a great one for times when you and your mate are away from each other)

- Print out a recipe they made that was delicious, and write on the back, "You are such an amazing cook – this was a wonderful dinner."

I love you!

These three words have more weight and fuss around them than any others. As I mentioned in Chapter 2, my family didn't say "I love you." We just took for granted that we loved each other, without the words. Yet over time I discovered that it meant a lot to me when a friend said the words. I learned to say the words to my best friends, and watched them light up. And I waited, so eagerly, for my then future husband to say it to me. I remember when he looked at me and told me "I love you" that first time. It was very special.

Saying "I love you" can still be special, even if you and your loved one have been saying those words to each other for years. But a lot of people let the words become routine, especially with their partner and family members. Maybe you and your partner still say it to each other when you leave in the morning, or before bed. But *how* do you say it? Is it an afterthought, something your mouth is saying while your mind is thinking about everything else you have to do?

It's time to reclaim "I love you," and make it part of the Words of Love and Support that you tell that special loved one who uses this love style.

By giving Words of Love and Support through affirmations, compliments, public encouragement, and your written word, you can really tell your loved one just how much you love them, and what they mean to you. Through practicing saying the love in your heart, your loved one will only love you more in response. As Sidney Madwed said,

> *"The finest gift you can give anyone is encouragement. Yet, almost no one gets the encouragement they need to grow to their full potential. If everyone received the encouragement they need to grow, the genius in most everyone would*

blossom and the world would produce abundance beyond the wildest dreams. We would have more than one Einstein, Edison, Schweitzer, Mother Theresa, Dr. Salk and other great minds in a century."

If your love style is Words of Love and Support

Most people know more about how to criticize and complain than how to speak supportively. This can make it tricky for you to get the Words of Love and Support you crave, especially since harsh words seem especially wounding. Here are some suggestions for you:

Ask for the verbal support you need. Be specific about what you do (and don't) want. It's often best to do this at a time when you *don't* need supportive words. That way if your loved one is reluctant or clumsy in delivering words, it's less likely to happen at a time when you feel vulnerable.

Give positive feedback when your loved one gives you the kind of verbal support you like. If they aren't a Words person themselves, they may not notice how special their words are for you.

Give Words of Love and Support. This helps set the tone of the relationship and encourages others to speak loving words. Pay particular attention to words that seem to move your loved one, or encourage them to praise you and others, and use them again.

Negotiate to increase praise in your relationship. Decide together to create a practice of praising everyone more, including each other. Then give each other praise for praising. And if your loved one uses another love style, also reward them using *their* love style.

By the way, praise doesn't always have to be verbal. Body Connection people often respond better to a nod and loving touch. And for some people, a *visual* connection such as meeting their eyes across the room and smiling at them means a lot.

CHAPTER 9

Deep Listening

Deep Listening is sometimes the love style that is hardest to give. People who use Deep Listening can feel alone, because most people think that merely listening is the same as listening *deeply*. Believe me, it's not.

I worked with a young man in his early 20's who felt very discouraged in his relationship with his fiancée. His fiancée was a charming, intelligent, beautiful woman, who loved him very much. Unfortunately, she had a habit of interrupting him when he was speaking. Because of this, he came to believe that, she didn't actually love or appreciate him. I helped them see that for her, offering her opinion was her way of showing love, while this young man needed to just be listened to.

We have all learned the polite ways to have conversations. Your friend talks about the book they just read, and as they are talking you hold your tongue until she pauses. Then you say your opinion of the book. Then she cuts in, and so on. There is a pace to when it is OK to speak after listening. It is deemed rude for someone to go on and on without allowing space for the other person to speak. I've known people who monopolize conversations like this at parties to the point where no one else can speak. They might as well be talking to a wall for all the input others can give!

Deep Listening is very different. Not only is it *not* rude for one person to talk for long periods of time; that's what you are there for! When you are in conversation with someone who has the love style of Deep Listening, you should be listening at least 80% of the time. That's right. 80% of the time you will simply be listening attentively and saying nothing.

Holding space

How you listen is very important, because even while you're not speaking, you are still communicating to your loved one that you are listening. How do you communicate this? Through body language, attitude, and what you think in your mind and feel in your heart, you let them know that you are holding space for them.

How to communicate that you are really listening

- **Let your body be still and relaxed.** Don't fidget or move around a lot. You can use shrugs and gestures when it's appropriate to do so. Keeping your body free of tension will communicate to your loved one that you are comfortable listening and are fully present.

- **Maintain eye contact.** Nothing says you are listening like keeping eye contact with your loved one. They can look away if it feels comfortable for them, but having you lock eyes with them when they look at you will communicate to them that you are listening deeply. Only do this if it's comfortable for you — otherwise you will communicate that you are uncomfortable!

- **Use interjections.** An often overlooked part of listening is using interjections, short sounds that let the other know you are listening. Examples of interjections are *hmm, aha,* and *oh.* Make sure to keep these from dominating your loved one's talking.

- **Let their words into your heart.** Deep Listening means opening your heart, and not just listening with your mind. Allow your emotions and your love to come forth while holding space. Let your love shine through your eyes. Really feel, deep inside, what it is that is being communicated to you.

When you speak, make it count

So if 80% of the time you are Deep Listening, what do you do with that other 20%? You get to let your loved one *know* you are listening, by speaking things that communicate that.

The specifics of what to say will vary from person to person, as each one of the people who use this love style have different needs around what they need to hear. The one thing they all need is to not hear judgment or criticism in your voice tone or words.

Non-judgment means being able to put aside your judgments and opinions. It means you must be able to understand what your loved one is going through, from *their* perspective. That's all they want! They want to know you can join them in their world, their struggles, and their love.

How to speak during Deep Listening

- **Communicate to them exactly what you heard them say in your own words.** By reflecting, you let them know that you heard them. Also, sometimes hearing something they've been thinking in someone else's words gives them new perspectives on it.

- **Ask questions.** By asking questions that are thoughtful, you can let your loved one know you have been listening, and are genuinely interested and curious about them and what they have been saying.

- **Share what you are feeling.** Sometimes, if you can't find the right words for a reflection or question, simply letting them know what feelings came up for you while they were speaking can be a powerful way to connect with them.

Stay present in the moment

It is important during Deep Listening that you stay present in the moment. Being in the present moment means having all of your body and mind in the room with your loved one.

How do you know if you are present? Each person has their own signs. I know I am present with my loved ones by feeling my feet on the ground, being able to remember the last things that were said, and feeling in touch with my emotions.

How do you know you are being present?

It is important to know yourself, and recognize the clues of when you are present and when you are not. Take a moment now and think of several times when you *knew* you were fully present in the here-and-now. Write a list of what you are aware of at those times:

- What emotions do you feel?

- What thoughts are in your mind?

- What sensations do you feel in your body?

- What are you aware of in the space around you?

- What senses are easiest for you to notice – touch, sight, smell, taste, hearing?

This will help you understand what it feels like for you when you are present, and when you are not.

What common factors do you notice in the situations where you are able to be present? What *is* there? What *isn't* there? A little detective work can often clue you in to factors that make it especially easy or difficult to be present. Many of my clients report that they have great difficulty staying present if there is a radio or TV going nearby, because it tends to distract them.

Now ask these questions again in various situations, for instance when watching TV or during church. You'll notice that sometimes you are aware of the here-and-now... while other times you're deep in thoughts and memories.

The truth is, you're always present to *something*... but what? Is it internal (what you are thinking and feeling), or external (what is going on around you, your loved one's responses)? Is your attention in the now, or in the past, or in the future?

Now that you have this knowledge, you can track yourself while you do Deep Listening. You'll be able to tell whether you are listening fully, or just pretending to. This can make all the difference for your loved one to *feel* deeply listened to.

Patience pays off

When you give the gift of Deep Listening, it may take a long time. Even if it doesn't, it might feel really long to you because the pace of the conversation is so different, with you speaking only 20% of the time.

Remember that by being fully present, Deep Listening, and speaking non-judgmentally, you are giving your loved one a gift that they have probably longed for a long time. Not many people have the patience to do this.

If your loved one has gone without Deep Listening for a long time, those first few conversations may be really long. Once your loved one gets a chance to talk and feels truly heard, they probably won't need to talk as long or as often.

Some people with the Deep Listening love style literally go *years* without anyone listening to them. One young man who came to see me for his first session talked for five hours straight! After being deeply listened to for five hours, he revealed that he had *never* felt fully listened to in his entire life. By the time he came in to see me, he felt so desperate to be heard that he was seriously considering suicide! Those five precious hours saved his life.

During a conversation when you are doing Deep Listening, stay aware of what you are communicating via your body language, facial expression, and your feelings, thoughts, and attention. Even though those last three are internal, your loved one will still read them via subtle shifts in your responses. By tracking yourself you can make sure that you stay present, and stay an effective deep listener.

Having patience can be hard, especially if you have a strong reaction to what is being said. You might really want to speak your mind, or react. I urge you to take a deep breath instead, and keep listening. Your loved one will have the amazing gift from you of being listened to deeply. And that will nurture their love for you. As the wise ones say, patience pays off!

If your love style is Deep Listening

Deep Listening is sometimes one of the harder love styles for others to deliver. Here are some suggestions to help you get the kind of love you need:

Ask for the kind of listening you want. A lot of times, this is the main thing they need: to hear and understand how much it means to you when they listen. Be specific about what kind of listening you want, so that they know that you want *listening,* not problem-solving or a lot of feedback.

Let people know when they listen in the ways you love. If their love style is not Deep Listening, they might be doing a *great* job of listening, yet think to themselves, *I'm lousy at supporting you because I don't have anything to say.*

A great way to give positive feedback is to say, "I really love it when you _____" (describe their behavior), "because it makes me feel _____" (now describe your positive emotions). This lets them know what is important *to you.*

You can also give examples of when other people listened in the ways you like. For instance, a client told me about being stressed out and going to her boss. The boss said "Do you want me to listen to you and let you express your emotions, or problem-solve?" This was a question that made her feel really loved, and knowing that helped me do an even better job of listening to her.

Help your loved ones give in the ways you want. If people listen in ways that *aren't* what you want, give them feedback in ways that will encourage them, rather than shut them down. Instead of saying, "Why don't you just listen to me the way I asked you to?" (which can sound like criticism, and discourage them from trying), say something like "I really appreciate you listening to me. I know you want to help with advice, and what I need right now is to just have you listen. Even more than advice, that will really help me to feel heard and loved."

If they still have trouble, give them something to do that is in their love style. For instance, if their strongest style is Body Connection, hold their hand or cuddle while they listen. If they prefer Practical Assistance, and have a hard time not giving you advice, either ask them to give you advice at another time, or request them to do something else for you that they know will be helpful.

Model Deep Listening.   A lot of people have never been around Deep Listening, which is why they don't know how to do it. If you simply provide a good example, a lot of people will quickly pick up the skills, especially if you encourage them.

Take an active listening class with your loved one.   If they're willing, a class can be a great way for them to learn and practice listening skills in a supportive environment. It can also help you learn to encourage their listening more effectively.

Set up times to practice.   This will ensure that the good intentions of the class turn into real-life skills that benefit you both.

CHAPTER 10

Conclusion

Congratulations! You have just learned six styles of giving and receiving loves that can improve *all* your close relationships, for the rest of your life.

At this point you understand that we all have preferred ways of giving and receiving love, and our needs in relationships tend to be based on our preferred love style(s).

I hope you've also figured out what love style or styles *you* favor. You've probably started to figure out which *expressions* of love in your favorite style work best for you.

You may even have started figuring out the love styles of your closest love ones.

Now what?

What should you *do* with all this important information about yourself and your loved ones? How can you apply this to your life, right now, creating closeness and connection through using the right love style with the right person?

Action steps

Expressing love in someone else's style requires knowing what it is. So your first task is to get good at figuring out people's love styles. It's impossible to move forward without knowing this.

In working with many clients, I've discovered that people become good at figuring out other people's love styles only by getting really familiar with this material. Below are some suggestions for how to learn and implement the love styles in your own life.

Reread this book

Even better, read it with your loved one. As you do, see if you can figure out the love styles of various people in your life, past and present.

Reread as many times as you need to really understand love styles *and use them.*

Figure out others people's love styles

This is often the most effective if you work with your loved ones to discover what works best for them. Share the information in this book with them. You might even lend or give them this book. Read it together. Ask them lots of questions. With your knowledge, and their input, together you can figure out their love style.

Another easy way to see if you are on the right track about someone's love style is by expressing your love from each of the love styles, and seeing which ones they really respond to. It can be frustrating when your love is not received, but the payoff is when you figure out what makes your loved one most happy!

I like to keep a little notebook, just for me, with what I notice other people in my life are giving or requesting in the love styles. This has really helped me become fluent, fluent enough to want to write this book for you!

Notice what you don't understand or resist

If you have trouble understanding a particular love style, or resist giving it, you may have an underlying issue that is interfering with your ability to give and receive love. Do the exercises in the Confusion and resistance section and feel your ability to love blossom. Especially if you've had trouble understanding or giving in the love style of a close loved one, they will *really* appreciate anything you do to enhance your ability to show them love in the ways that mean so much to them.

Practice!

Practice really does make perfect, especially in loving. The more you notice yourself and others using the love styles, the more you request love in your love style, and the more you encourage your loved ones to do so, the faster you'll get fluent in all the styles and the more your relationships will improve.

In fact when people feel deeply loved around you, you may find your biggest problem is having so many people want to spend time with you every chance they get!

Living the love styles can change your life

The love styles have helped hundreds of my clients revive failing relationships, solve their family problems, save friendships, and deepen their love. They have made me a better coach, wife, mother, and friend. I am so thankful to know this material, and share it with you.

What I and my friends, loved ones, and clients have discovered is that *using the love styles can improve ALL your relationships.* When both you and your loved ones are getting the love you need, longstanding problems often become minor or just disappear. Love and happiness bloom, and motivate you to love even more.

When emotional needs get met, you and your loved one feel more whole and balanced. From that place, no longer feeling needy or desperate, you can make much better decisions. You become kinder, and less likely to do something thoughtless or make relationship mistakes. Because you are nourished in your relationships, you have plenty of energy for yourself and an abundance of love to give. And you can give fully – your time, your words, your gifts, your touch, your help, your ear. When you give, you can do it with full presence and from your heart.

This is the gift I offer to you! I hope that this book has touched you, and will allow you to make good changes to your life, and to become someone who lives from your understanding of the love styles. Learning to use the love styles is a rewarding journey, and I wish you luck and blessings, to you and all your loved ones.

Other books by Linda Johnson

<u>Intuition: Your Most Powerful Tool</u>

Develop your intuition and notice how quickly you become more happy, healthy and wealthy. This simple program helps you understand the source of your intuition and strengthen this critical skill to be more successful at work, in relationships and at home.

http://amzn.to/2eiZlpV

<u>How to Talk to Your Kids and Grandkids: 10 Secrets to being the Grandmothr Everyone Adores</u>

This guide explores the 10 ways to talk to your kids, as well as fun tips for opening up conversations with your grandkids.

http://amzn.to/2ejBNFR

Deborah Williams and Linda A. Johnson

How to Talk to your Kids and Grandkids

10 Secrets to Being the Grandmother Everyone Adores

Beginning Meditation for Busy People: How to Get More Done, Feel Less Stressed and Be Happier

Stress has become a large part of our every day life, making us anxious, exhausted and sometimes even affecting our health. This simple meditation book takes you step-by-step through meditation practices that are designed with a busy lifestyle in mind.

http://amzn.to/2do11n7

The 7 Secrets to Happiness: How to Bring Joy into Your Everyday Life

Happiness seems like a universal desire – lots of people are searching for it, and few really find it. The 7 Secrets of Happiness gives you a clear map for the journey. With simple and powerful life strategies you can easily incorporate into your everyday life to feel more fulfilled, less anxious, and happier!

http://amzn.to/2cPnBBc

Reviews are very important for the success of a book. If you enjoyed *Giving for their Love Language: The Secrets to Gifts They Love*, please leave a review. Even a few words helps. Thank you!

www.ingramcontent.com/pod-product-compliance
Lightning Source LLC
Chambersburg PA
CBHW070119290526
45789CB00005B/2062